GRACE BANKER
AND HER
HELLO GIRLS
ANSWER THE CALL

THE HEROIC STORY OF WWI TELEPHONE OPERATORS

written by

CLAUDIA FRIDDELL

illustrated by

ELIZABETH BADDELEY

The excerpts in blue type and in speech bubbles are from Grace's diaries and interviews.

CALKINS CREEK

AN IMPRINT OF BOYDS MILLS & KANE

New York

Grace Banker opened the newspaper on a brisk December morning in 1917—

The world was at war, and General John J. Pershing, the commander of US troops across the Atlantic, was calling for female telephone operators to join the fight against Germany.

Grace knew she had just what the army's Signal Corps needed—
   college education—check
   fluency in French—check
   telephone operator expertise—check
Along with thousands of female telephone operators
known across the country as *Hello Girls,*
Grace answered the call and crossed her fingers.

*Full of youthful enthusiasm,
I enlisted.*

Women had never been allowed in the army—
they weren't even allowed to vote!

But that didn't stop Grace. She was used to marching
in a man's world. Few women had been to college,
and few had jobs outside the home, but Grace was
twenty-five years old and already training other
switchboard operators.

When she opened her mail from the Signal Corps, Grace couldn't believe her eyes—not only did she get the call to serve overseas with the first group of thirty-three female operators, but Grace was named their chief operator.

After two months of classes . . . drills . . .
uniform fittings . . . and oath swearing . . .
Grace led her Signal Corps Girls onto the
troop ship *Celtic*—and into the world of war.

With faces glued to port holes and doors
watched the Statue of Liberty fade from sight.
For the first time suddenly realized what a responsability [sic]
I have on my young shoulders.

Grace and her girls had plenty of grit. They kept their cool outside Liverpool when their ship, the perfect target for a German submarine attack, was stuck on a sandbar.

They kept their cool in the English Channel when their ferry, bumped by a patrol boat and caught in a submarine net, was trapped in fog.

And they kept their cool on their first night in Paris when German air-raid sirens blasted through the streets, forcing them out of their beds and into the dark.

ALERTE! ALERTE! ALERTE! ALERTE!

The minute the Signal Corps Girls started plugging in cords and connecting calls at General Pershing's headquarters in France, calls poured in from some homesick doughboys missing the voices of their mothers, sisters, wives, and sweethearts.

Chief Operator Grace Banker was all business when she was on duty. There were rules to follow, schedules to make, problems to solve, and curfews to meet.

Over here a Chief operator has a twenty four hour job. . . . Never spent more time at the office and never enjoyed anything more. My girls work like beavers.

Lt. Riser came to dinner to-night. He was very late. . . . I set the alarm clock off under his chair to let him see how late it was. Fortunately he took it as a good joke.

When she was *off* duty Grace was the life of the party! There were villages to explore, dances to enjoy, dinners to share, and pranks to pull.

Grace made the most of her time away from the boards, but when General Pershing called for her to command the switchboards at his new headquarters, Grace gathered her girls and headed toward the front.

With gas masks and helmets hanging on their chairs, the Signal Corps Girls pulled the plugs at lightning speed, keeping the combat commands moving.

Soaking rainstorms, leaky barracks, sore backs, tired eyes—conditions were rough for the operators, but Grace never complained and never forgot how rough it was for the brave soldiers in the battlefield trenches.

The determined doughboys surprised the world and pushed the Germans back. Grace and her girls packed up and once again advanced alongside the soldiers.

They never flinched when German planes dropped bombs overhead, explosions thundered nearby, and shrapnel landed at their feet.

Nothing could shake the Signal Corps Girls from their stations. Every new call could save lives. Any missed command could lose the battle.

Suddenly the shrapnel which had gone up began to come down. We made for cover but not before one piece fell right beside me. I didn't realize how dangerous it was . . . we might have been killed.

Different accents to decipher, countless orders to relay, secret codes to remember—Grace's Signal Corps Girls connected hundreds of orders in an hour, thousands of commands in a day.

Two hours sleep in two days but didn't notice it. . . . The names of all the places here and further fronts beyond are known under code names. Waterfall Buster Bonehead Podunk Jam, etc., all mean some place very definite. The codes are changed frequently so I have to keep up on everything.

General Pershing depended on Grace and her Signal Corps Girls when he moved the First Army to a top secret location.

Like the conductor of an orchestra, Grace directed her girls from the top of a crate. With fingers flying over the fighting lines' switchboards, the operators barely noticed the bitter winds or leaky barracks.

Our office is most primitive. Three switchboards, not an other stick of furniture. There was one large packing box so I decided to use that as a combined chair and desk. Once on top I felt as though I were up on a mountain. I wouldnt exchange this bare office for any other. I love it here.

When a wood stove turned over, fire raged through the camp. The spreading flames and burning barracks couldn't stop Grace's girls from plugging on. The general's commands came through their lines— they couldn't miss a call!

When flames engulfed their barracks, the Signal Corps Girls wouldn't budge. The commanders threatened court martial if they didn't leave at once! The operators had no choice—they had to leave their switchboards.

For the first time during the war, General Headquarters lost contact with the front. But not for long—thirty minutes later, the gritty girls rushed back to their switchboards, keeping the battle commands moving.

Thanks to the doughboys' push on the front lines and the Signal Corps Girls' pull on the phone lines, Pershing's troops won the battle that would end the war.

At the eleventh hour, on the eleventh day, of the eleventh month, an armistice was signed to end the war. Phone lines were damaged, but final orders had to go out to all the battlefront commanders.

A captain of the Signal Corps picked up Grace's phone and made an urgent call—

On May 22, 1919, Chief Operator Grace Banker received one last call—this time to reward her with the Distinguished Service Medal "for exceptionally meritorious and distinguished services."

Headlines across America spread the news that Grace Banker was the first woman soldier to earn the US Army's highest honor for someone not in combat. Grace wore her medal proudly on behalf of all her brave comrades in the Signal Corps.

THE UNITED STATES OF AMERICA

TO ALL WHO SHALL SEE THESE PRESENTS, GREETING:

THIS IS TO CERTIFY THAT

THE PRESIDENT OF THE UNITED STATES OF AMERICA

PURSUANT TO ACT OF CONGRESS APPROVED JULY 9, 1918

HAS AWARDED TO

Grace D. Banker

THE DISTINGUISHED SERVICE MEDAL

FOR

EXCEPTIONALLY MERITORIOUS AND DISTINGUISHED SERVICES

IN THE PERFORMANCE OF DUTIES OF GREAT RESPONSIBILITY AS

Chief Operator, Signal Corps Exchange at GHQ A.E.F., and later at First Army Headquarters, in the World War.

GIVEN UNDER MY HAND AT THE CITY OF WASHINGTON

THIS *thirteenth* DAY OF *January*, 1926

Dwight O. Dauh

Robert Dau

There are many who saw far more service than I, and many who earned medals even if they did not receive them. Mine I consider as a tribute to the girls who worked under me at the First Army and to the Signal Corps men operators scattered throughout France in the tiny field offices.

Grace Banker may not have marched with the troops, but she and the Signal Corps Girls served their country—right in step with the thousands of soldiers who returned home as heroes, ready to make their way in a new world.

AFTERWORD

In 1919, Grace returned to a new and busy life of her own. After working for the YWCA, she married and raised four children. She saved detailed diaries, letters, postcards, and mementos, but like many World War I veterans, she packed away her keepsakes and rarely spoke about her wartime experiences.

The echoes of war never completely left her, however. Grace remained a devoted sister to her brother Eugene, who served in World War I in the 77th Field Artillery, 4th Division, and suffered from gas poisoning. She also cared for a son who was injured while serving in World War II.

A SOLDIER'S POEM

Sing a song of six sous
toll for conversation,
three and thirty phone girls
here to help the nation.
When the camera snapped them
they didn't budge or fuss,
isn't that a proof they're soldiers
just like us.

PRESENTED
TO
GRACE D. BANKER
BY
THE CITIZENS OF
PASSAIC, NEW JERSEY

MEMENTO
ONE OPERATING UNITS...
NAL CORPS
HRISTMAS...
FRANCE
1918

COMMERCE DE FRANCE · CHAMBRES DE
BON POUR
5
CENTIMES

20
CENTIMES

S, FRANCE

A young Grace Banker

One fights best with patience and
with understanding.
—Grace Banker

Grace Banker's Timeline

October 25, 1892: Grace Banker is born in Passaic, New Jersey.

1915: Grace graduates from Barnard College in New York City with majors in French and history.

June 1915–January 1918: Grace is an instructor at an AT&T operators' school in New York City.

November 8, 1917: General Pershing asks the Signal Corps to form a unit of 100 American operators who also speak French for telephone duty overseas.

January 12, 1918: The first group of Signal Corps operator candidates begins six weeks of training.

February 15, 1918: Grace is appointed Chief Operator of the 1st Telephone Unit of the United States Signal Corps.

March 6, 1918: Grace departs with the first unit of Signal Corps operators for duty in France on the troop ship *Celtic*.

March 27, 1918: Grace begins work as chief operator at General Pershing's headquarters in Chaumont, France.

August 25, 1918: Grace and five operators arrive at First Army Headquarters for the St. Mihiel Offensive in Ligny-en-Barrois. The operators connect calls between the front lines and General Pershing's battlefield command center.

Grace Banker (*front row, middle*) and her First Telephone Operators Unit, Signal Corps,
at Square de l'Opéra-Louis-Jouvet, Paris, 1918

September 20, 1918: Grace and her operators move to Souilly with the First Army for the Meuse-Argonne Offensive. They connect calls 24 hours a day amid German aerial bombings and in freezing conditions.

October 30, 1918: A fire burns the barracks and nearly destroys the camp. For the first time during the war, headquarters has no communication with the front. The operators refuse to leave their switchboards until ordered to leave.

November 11, 1918: The armistice is signed at 11:00 a.m., ceasing all fighting, after the Allied forces defeat the Germans. The Signal Corps captain uses Grace's phone to relay the ceasefire order.

March–May 1919: Grace serves as chief operator at President Wilson's temporary residence in Paris during the first peace conference.

With gas masks and helmets hanging from their chairs, Grace Banker, Berthe Hunt, and Tootsie Fresnel (*left to right*) connect calls to French battlefields from General Pershing's First Army Headquarters in Souilly, France.

May 22, 1919: Grace is awarded the Distinguished Service Medal in Coblenz (later Koblenz), Germany, where she is stationed with the Army of Occupation.

September 1919: Grace sails home to America after twenty months of service. When the Signal Corps women return, they learn they are considered civilians and do not qualify for the benefits awarded all other veterans, including those who never served in France.

1924: Grace and General Pershing meet at a WWI memorial dedication event in Grace's hometown of Passaic, New Jersey.

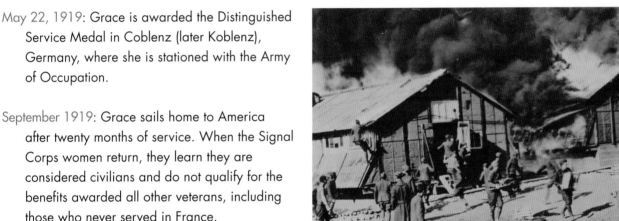

On October 30, 1918, the barracks where the Signal Corps worked and lived caught fire.

September 17, 1960: Grace Banker dies in Scarsdale, New York.

1977: After a nearly sixty-year battle led by Signal Corps operator Merle Egan Anderson, US Congress passes legislation that recognizes Grace and the female Signal Corps soldiers as veterans. This gives them the distinction of being America's first official women soldiers.

1977–1979: For two years, attorney Mark Hough helps the surviving Signal Corps women operators apply individually for their Victory Medals, proof of their military service. These newly recognized veterans never receive the bonuses paid long before to others. Since Grace died in 1960, she never received her long-awaited Victory Medal.

2018: The National World War I Museum and Memorial opens the Grace D. Banker special exhibit.

The Fight Back Home

When Grace Banker returned to America after the war, the world had definitely changed. In 1920—the year when the last of the Signal Corps Girls came home—the Nineteenth Amendment passed, giving women the right to vote. Unfortunately, the Signal Corps Girls returned home to disappointing news. These women—who had loyally taken the army oath, proudly worn uniforms, faithfully followed regulations, and bravely served on the front lines to defend their country and win the war—learned that they were denied veterans' benefits.

Merle Egan was another Signal Corps operator with a leadership role. She supervised the telephone lines at the Paris Peace Conference following the war. When she returned home to Helena, Montana, she too settled into a new life and married. Her husband, H. R. Anderson, wrote to the army to learn how his wife could receive her victory medal, but was told the Signal Corps women operators were considered civilians, not soldiers, even though they were recruited, uniformed, and paid by the army.

Merle Egan Anderson made it her lifelong mission to get veterans' benefits and rights for the 223 Signal Corps telephone operators who had faithfully served their country. Yet it was not a quick or easy mission. More than fifty bills introduced in Congress over a period of almost six decades failed to pass. Finally, with the help of Mark Hough, a devoted volunteer lawyer, the Signal Corps operators won the fight. Congress passed a bill giving them full veteran status in 1977, making them the first female soldiers to serve in the US Army. Sadly, only Merle and thirty other Signal Corps operators were still alive to receive their Victory Medals and veteran recognition. Grace Banker had died seventeen years earlier, in 1960.

Grace Banker with her Distinguished Service Medal pinned to a new uniform she purchased in Paris after the Armistice

Number, Please!

If you were to ask every girl in my party about her hardships, I know she would answer that she had none worth mentioning—and that if she was afraid, at least she never said anything about it—and that her work overseas helped her in every way and made her a bigger person than she was before. —Grace Banker

- More than 7,600 women telephone operators volunteered to serve.
- 350 female operators received training and official army uniforms, including ID tags in case of death.
- 223 operators were assigned to 6 units and sailed for France, where those closest to the front got gas masks and steel helmets.
- Grace's unit of Signal Corps operators took a 12-day voyage overseas on the *Celtic*.
- Each Signal Corps Girl connected an average of 300 calls an hour.
- By the end of the war, the Signal Corps Girls had connected more than 26 million calls!
- 20 countries gave women the vote before the United States did.
- It took the American women's suffrage movement 72 years to get the vote.
- It took almost 60 years for the Signal Corps telephone Girls to get their Victory Medals for service in World War I.

Sisterhood

Thanks to the YWCA (Young Women's Christian Association), the Signal Corps operators received help from other women while they served in the army. YWCA women provided housing and meals, organized entertainment, and enforced army regulations for the Signal Corps operators. When Grace Banker returned home after the war, she worked for the YWCA.

A World of Firsts

- The First World War, World War I, was originally called the Great War.
- It was the first war to use modern technologies: machine guns, submarines, airplanes, armored tanks, and poison gas.
- Telephones were widely used for the first time in WWI to connect general headquarters with battlefronts.
- General Pershing's American Expeditionary Forces (AEF) were called the "First Army." Grace Banker was the chief operator of Pershing's First Army Headquarters.
- Grace Banker was the first chief operator to lead the first unit of Army Signal Corps operators to go overseas.
- Grace and her operators were the first unit of women soldiers.
- Grace Banker was the first and only woman operator in the Signal Corps (out of 16,000 Signal Corps officers) to receive the Army Distinguished Service Medal.

How Did a Switchboard Operator Operate in World War I?

- The telephone operator who worked the telephone switchboard wore a headset.
- The switchboard had phone jacks and pairs of plugs.
- Each jack had a light above it.
- When the caller's telephone receiver was lifted off the latch of the phone, the jack on the switchboard lit up.
- Alerted, the operator plugged a cord into that jack.
- The caller told the operator at the central office where he/she wanted to call.
- The operator then plugged the opposite end of the cord into the circuit jack of the requested location to connect the call.
- The operator checked back periodically during the call.
- Often the Signal Corps operators served as a translator between French and English callers.
- When the receiver was placed back on the latch of the phone, the operator disconnected the call.

Bibliography

All quotations in the book can be found in the following sources marked with an asterisk (*).

AT&T "Famous Chief Operator Dies" *Long Lines* (company newsletter), February, 1961.

* Banker, Grace. *Diary: Signal Corps Days in the A.E.F., 1918–1919.* Typewritten transcript of the diary of Grace Banker Paddock. (From Carolyn Timbie's personal collection).

* Banker, Grace [Grace Banker Paddock]. "I Remember…" Personal recollections of Grace Banker. (From Carolyn Timbie's personal collection).

* Banker, Grace [Grace Banker Paddock]. "I Was a Hello Girl." *Yankee* Magazine, AHC, File: 71. March 1974.

* Banker, Grace [Mrs. Eugene H. Paddock]. "Mrs. Eugene Paddock, Honored in the World War, Tells of Some Experiences." *Scarsdale Inquirer* 13, no. 16 (May 29, 1931). news.hrvh.org/veridian/?a=d&d=scarsdalein-quire19310529.2.48.

* Banker, Grace. [Grace Banker Paddock]. *My Experiences as a Chief Operator in France,* November 1937. AT&T publication, (From Carolyn Timbie's personal collection).

Boissoneault, Lorraine. "Women on the Frontlines of WWI Came to Operate Telephones." Interview with Elizabeth Cobbs. smithsonianmag.com/history/women-front-lines-wwi-came-operate-telephones-180962687/.

Cobbs, Elizabeth. *The Hello Girls: America's First Women Soldiers.* Cambridge, MA: Harvard University Press, 2017.

Cobbs, Elizabeth. Interviews conducted by the author, Claudia Friddell, 2017–2019.

Frahm, Jill. "Women Telephone Operators in World War I France." nsa.gov/Portals/70/documents/about/cryptologic-heritage/historical-figures-publications/publications/pre-wwii/women-phone-operators-in-wwi-france.pdf.

Gavin, Lettie. *American Women in World War I: They Also Served.* Louisville, CO: University Press of Colorado, 1997.

Hanshew, Annie. "Merle Egan Anderson: Montana's 'Hello Girl.'" Nov. 11, 2014. montanawomenshistory.org/merle-egan-anderson-montanas-hello-girl/.

*Marshall, Marguerite Mooers. "How the Signal Corps Girls 'Stayed on the Job,' Told by Grace D. Banker, D.S.M." *New York Evening World*, September 9, 1919.

* Pershing, General John, (Cablegram), National Archives at College Park, MD, Record Group 111 Entry (PI–155) 45 Records of the Office of the Chief Signal Officer. Correspondence, 1897–1942, Box 396, File 231.3, Telephone Operators (Folder No. 1) 1917–1919.

Raines, Rebecca Robbins. "Getting the Message Through." In *A Branch History of the U.S. Army Signal Corps.* Washington, D.C.: U.S. Army Center of Military History, 1996, pp. 165–200.

Stars and Stripes articles: "Uncle Sam Presents 'Hello, Girls!'" (March 29, 1918, p. 1, col. 3). "Six Hello Girls Help First Army" (October 4, 1918, p. 6, col. 2).

Theres, James. *The Hello Girls Documentary.* Lincoln Penny Films, MJRvisuals, DVD. 2018.

Timbie, Carolyn (Grace Banker's granddaughter). Interviews conducted by the author, Claudia Friddell, 2017–2019.

YWCA, *Annual Report, Signal Corps Work in France,* 1918, Box 7, Folder 16.

Zeiger, Susan, *In Uncle Sam's Service: Women Workers with the American Expeditionary Force, 1917–1919.* Ithaca, NY: Cornell University Press, 1999.

Picture Credits

Artist's Note

There are a lot of historical details in this book. Before I begin to have fun creating imaginative illustrations, I have to do a lot of research to make sure I am drawing those details accurately. As it so happens, I live in Kansas City, Missouri—the home of the National World War I Museum and Memorial (theworldwar.org). When I first began working on this book, I paid a visit to the museum. They have everything you could possibly want to see related to WWI, but most importantly for me, Grace Banker's actual uniform and helmet! I was able to take my sketchbook and sit and draw her uniform standing right in front of me. Toward the end of working on this book, my city (and probably yours, too) went into quarantine. The museums closed and I was unable to visit and draw. Fortunately, the WWI museum has a huge online collections database. You can visit the website and type in "switchboard" to see drawings and photographs of the real switchboards they used during the war. I looked at photographs, postcards, and even diary entries before ever putting pencil to paper. I love to be creative and have fun getting messy with ink and paint, but the real work always starts with the research.

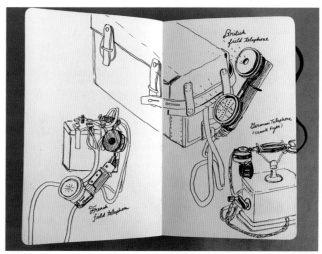

Acknowledgments

Thanks to my agent, Rachel Orr; Jonathan Casey and Doran Cart at the Edward Jones Research Center at the National World War I Museum and Memorial in Kansas City; and Eric Vanslander at the National Archives and Records Administration, College Park, Maryland. Special thanks to the gracious and generous Elizabeth Cobbs, whose book *The Hello Girls* inspired me to write about Grace Banker and the Signal Corps Girls of World War I. And, I am forever grateful to Carolyn Timbie for welcoming me into her grandmother's world. I cherish the memory of sitting together at her family's lakeside cabin late into the night, sorting through Grace Banker's diaries, photos, and mementos.

Pages from the artist's sketchbook

For Grace's family—
most especially her devoted granddaughter,
Carolyn Timbie, who honors her grandmother's
memory and legacy with a grace of her own.
And for all the heroic American women who
have loyally sacrificed and served their country,
many without recognition or commendation.
—CF

For all the Hello Girls who left seeking adventure
and returned heroes
—EB

Text copyright © 2021 by Claudia Friddell
Illustrations copyright © 2021 by Elizabeth Baddeley

For information about permission to reproduce selections
from this book, please contact permissions@bmkbooks.com.

Calkins Creek
An imprint of Boyds Mills & Kane,
a division of Astra Publishing House
calkinscreekbooks.com
Printed in China

ISBN: 978-1-68437-350-5 (hc) / 978-1-63592-371-1 (eBook)
Library of Congress Control Number: 2020933250

First edition
10 9 8 7 6 5 4 3 2 1

Design by Barbara Grzeslo
The text is set in Futura.
The artwork was created with a combination of ink, acrylic, and digital media.

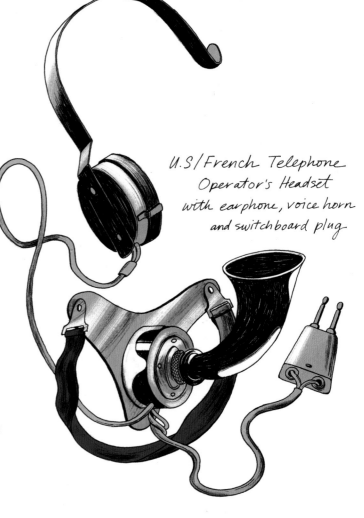

U.S/French Telephone
Operator's Headset
with earphone, voice horn
and switchboard plug